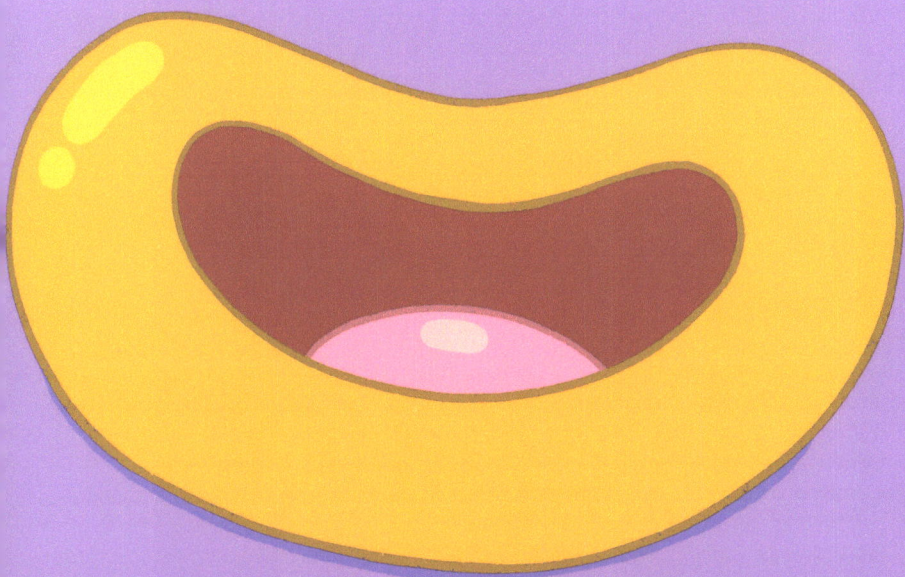

Obscure & Company LLC
1839 Winnetka Ave.
Northfield, IL 60093
https://www.obscureandco.com

ISBN: 979-8-9857620-7-5

Printed in the United States of America
First Edition

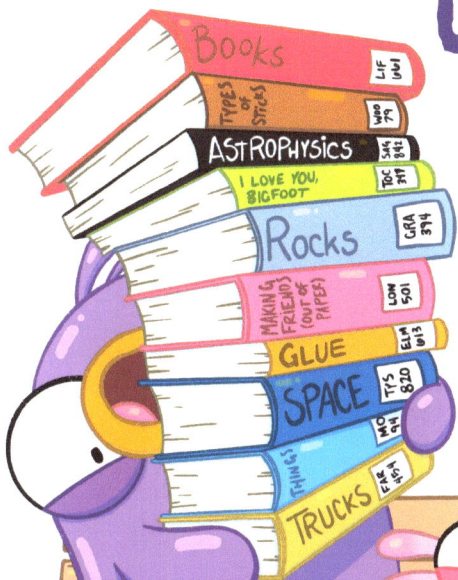

CHILLY
TEMPS THAT FREEZE MY BOOTY

PAIL IS A BUCKET TO HOLD OUR SAND

MORNING TIME GET OUT OF BED

ANT IS A SIX-LEGGED PICNIC PESTER

AUNT IS THE WIFE OF MY UNCLE LESTER

FLEE FROM A CHARGING, ANGRY YAK

FLARE IS THE LIGHT FROM MY SINKING BOAT

COARSE
LIKE THE
CURLY HAIR
OF A SHEEP

NIGHT WHEN STARS COME OUT TO PLAY

KNIGHT TO KEEP DRAGONS AWAY

TOE IS A FINGER FOR MY FEET

TOW WHEN I PULL YOUR CAR FROM THE STREET

MAY I HAVE A TURN?

OF COURSE!

I'M THE ONE WHO WON WITH A TWO-STEP FLOW, DROPPED TWO LINES FAST, 'CAUSE YOU'RE MOVIN' TOO SLOW. CAME TO THE STAGE WITH RHYMES TO EXPLORE, GOT BARS FOR DAYS— YOU CAN'T HANDLE FOUR MORE. YOU SPIT WEAK HEAT? I'LL SETTLE THE SCORE— I BROUGHT ONE BEAT, BUT I'M LEAVIN' WITH FOUR!

THAT WAS
AMAZING!

FOR REY, CORA,
AND THOR

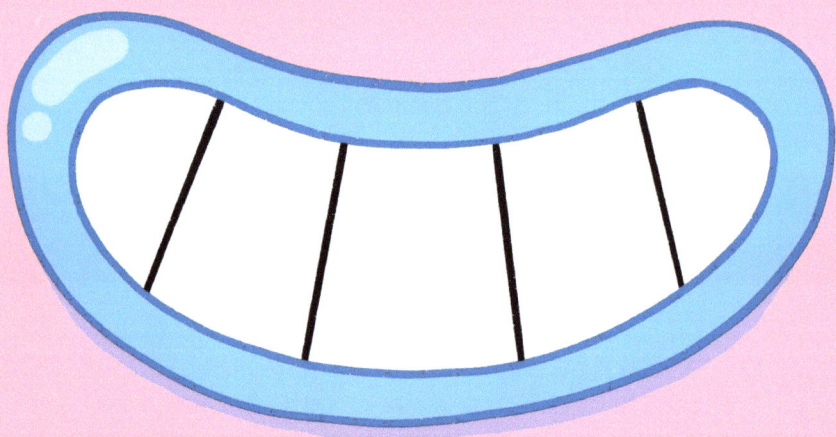

www.ingramcontent.com/pod-product-compliance
Lightning Source LLC
Chambersburg PA
CBHW041808040426

42449CB00001B/3